Records of
IMPEACHMENT

Introduction by
Michael K. Honey

MILESTONE DOCUMENTS IN THE NATIONAL ARCHIVES

National Archives and Records Administration

Washington, DC

Published for the
National Archives and Records Administration
by the
National Archives Trust Fund Board
1987

Library of Congress Cataloging-in-Publication Data

Honey, Michael.
    Records of impeachment.

    (Milestone documents in the National Archives)
      1. Impeachments — United States — History — Sources.
2. Johnson, Andrew, 1808–1875 — Impeachment — History —
Sources.   3. Nixon, Richard M. (Richard Milhous),
1913–   — Impeachment — History — Sources. I. United
States. National Archives and Records Administration.
II. Title. III. Series.
KF5075.H66   1986   342.73'062   86-16307
ISBN 0-911333-49-5   347.30262

AN INTRODUCTION

On August 9, 1974, Richard Nixon became the first President of the United States to resign from office. He did so in order to avoid impeachment by the House of Representatives and subsequent trial by the Senate for high crimes and misdemeanors he allegedly committed while occupying the highest office in the land.

A bill of particulars against the President, compiled by the House Judiciary Committee following its nationally televised hearings in July 1974, threatened Nixon with impeachment. The hearings had revealed a widespread pattern of abuse of Presidential power, including the use of "dirty tricks," wiretapping, and persecution of political opponents. Investigations had focused on the efforts of the President and his advisors to cover up a burglary conducted against the Democratic National Committee at the Watergate apartment building by men working under cover for the Committee to Re-Elect the President.

By voting to adopt three articles of impeachment against the President, the House Judiciary Committee for the first time in the 20th century attempted to take legal action to put a check on the use of power by the Chief Executive. The committee charged Nixon with using the Presidential office to obstruct the administration of justice in an attempt to cover up the Watergate affair; with unlawful utilization of federal agencies to violate the constitutional rights of citizens through wiretapping, surveillance, and various tactics of intimidation; and with ignoring the subpoenas of a congressional committee. The committee also considered, but failed to adopt, two articles charging the President with illegally bombing Cambodia and the illegal use of campaign funds.

The threatened impeachment and Nixon's resignation from office profoundly shook the confidence of the American people in their government and revealed a constitutional crisis that had grown out of the expansion of power in the hands of the President at the expense of the delegated powers of Congress. The "Imperial Presidency," as historian Arthur Schlesinger called it, resulted from a broad assumption of power by a series of Presidents from the period of the New Deal in the 1930s to the Vietnam war in the 1960s and early 1970s. Critics felt that this assumption of power by the Chief Executive threatened the structure of democratic government.

THE WHITE HOUSE

WASHINGTON

August 9, 1974

Dear Mr. Secretary:

I hereby resign the Office of President of the
United States.

Sincerely,

Richard Nixon

11.35 AM

HK

The Honorable Henry A. Kissinger
The Secretary of State
Washington, D.C. 20520

President Richard Nixon's letter of resignation, 1974, is the first presidential resignation in U.S. history. An act of March 1, 1792, provides that a President or Vice President shall tender his resignation to the Secretary of State. (RG 59, National Archives)

The Watergate affair focused public attention on the little-used impeachment provisions of the Constitution, which establish Congress as a court of last resort to challenge public officials who violate the law or in some way misuse the public trust. Impeachment can be and has been used by Congress against a variety of federal officials.* Perhaps the most important

---

*The House has impeached 13 officials, including 1 Cabinet officer, 1 Senator, 1 President, and 10 federal judges. The 11 impeachments tried by the Senate produced 4 convictions—all of them of federal judges—6 acquittals, and 1 dismissal.

purpose of the impeachment process, however, is to provide a means whereby Congress can challenge misuses of power by the executive and judicial branches, thereby sustaining the system of checks and balances between the three branches of government. Without the power of impeachment, the legislative branch would have few sanctions to stop federal executive and judicial officials from acting "above the law." '

The Constitution stipulates the impeachment powers of Congress. Article I, section 2 (5) provides the House with the sole power to impeach the President, that is, to draw up and adopt a bill of particulars justifying removal from office. Section 3 (6) requires the Senate to try all impeachments, designates the Chief Justice of the Supreme Court as the presiding officer when the trial is of an impeached President, and requires a two-thirds vote of the Senate to convict a person of impeachment. Section 3 (7) specifies that punishment after conviction shall be removal from office and disqualification to hold any federal office; it also states that the convicted party remains subject to trial and punishment in the civil courts. Article II, section 2 (1) bars the President from using his power to grant pardons as a means of escaping impeachment proceedings. Beyond these specific guidelines, the framers of the Constitution left it to Congress to determine the procedures it would use to carry out impeachment by the House and trial by the Senate.

To some extent, they also left it to Congress to decide the nature of impeachable offenses. Article II, section 4, defines the nature of impeachable offenses, stating, "the President, Vice President and all civil Officers of the United States, shall be removed from Office on Impeachment for, and Conviction of, Treason, Bribery, or other high Crimes and Misdemeanors." However, the Constitution's authors did not clearly define what they meant by high crimes and misdemeanors. Alexander Hamilton and James Madison wrote that this term could include abuses of the public trust as well as illegal conduct by Presidential subordinates, while George Mason allowed that "corruption" could be an impeachable offense. In the Watergate case, the defenders of the President argued against these broad interpretations, contending that the House had to find specific evidence of a serious criminal offense in order to impeach. The resignation of President Nixon brought to a halt the proceedings begun by the House Judiciary Committee and prevented the House from further defining impeachable offenses. President Gerald Ford's subsequent pardon of Nixon for all cirmes he may have committed or taken part in while in office prevented a further legal test of the extent to which a President may be held legally accountable for his actions in office.

Because the proceedings against President Nixon remained incomplete, historical precedent for the use of congressional impeachment power against the Chief Executive still rests largely on impeachment proceedings completed more than 100 years before the Nixon Presidency, during the tenure of President Andrew Johnson. As in the congressional conflict with President Nixon, proceedings against Johnson came at the end of a long and divisive war and in the midst of unresolved disputes over what congressional critics considered to be the misuse of the powers of the Presidency. Unlike President Nixon, Johnson stood trial before the Senate. The proceedings went on for more than 2 months in the spring of 1868 and gripped the nation much as did the Watergate hearings in the summer of 1974.

The impeachment of Andrew Johnson resulted from a series of conflicts between the President and Congress over the reconstruction of the nation following the termination of the American Civil War in April 1865. In the remaining months of 1865, with Congress in recess, President Johnson granted amnesties to most Confederate leaders and established provisional governments for the purpose of bringing the southern states back into the Union. Johnson required only that these governments adopt the 13th amendment abolishing slavery, repudiate the Confederate war debt and seccession, and be composed of delegates swearing allegiance to the federal government. This minimal policy of Reconstruction, which required no redistribution of political power or wealth in the South, followed a similar program adopted by Abraham Lincoln before his assassination in April. Like Lincoln, Johnson asserted that the President's war powers gave him the authority to reconstruct the Union without congressional assistance.

However, Johnson's Reconstruction program placed him on a collision course with the Republican-dominated Congress, which regarded the new governments he established in the South as an attempt to subvert the victories won by the Union during the war. During President Johnson's control of the Reconstruction process in 1865, the white South elected prominent ex-Confederates, including former Confederate Vice President Alexander Stephens of Georgia, to the U.S. Senate and other high offices. As the results of the abolition of slavery, under which Congress had counted black males as only three-fifths of a man for the purposes of federal representation, the South gained 15 more representatives to Congress. Yet because blacks remained disenfranchised and the old plantation aristocracy remained in power, no possibility for establishing a two-party system in the South existed. Thus, after the bloodiest war in U.S. history, Presidential Reconstruction restored to power many of the same Democratic politicians and large land holders who had taken the South out of the union in 1861.

Congress regarded Johnson's support for the governments in the South as betrayal of the Union. Radical Republican supporters of racial equality took a similar view of Johnson's refusal to enact any measures besides the 13th amendment to provide for black rights. Johnson's support for white supremacy and the right of state and local governments to determine the nature of race relations, along with the restoration of the old plantation and political elite of the South to power, encouraged the southern states to adopt quickly an array of laws to control the ex-slaves. These "black codes" imposed racial segregation and made blacks ineligible to vote, serve on juries, or exercise other citizenship rights. At the same time, the South established a system of economic servitude similar to that of slavery.

Republican leaders denounced the new regimes in the South, but Johnson, a Tennessee Democrat and former slaveholder, announced in December 1865 that every southern state except Texas had met his requirements for rejoining the Union and declared the Union to be restored. Not surprisingly, when the Republican-controlled Congress reconvened in the same month, Johnson's program met fierce opposition. Indeed, the Congress refused to seat the southern delegates elected under Johnson's program. Instead, it established a 15-member joint committee on Reconstruction for the purpose of making alternate plans for reorganizing the South.

The return of Confederates to power in the South, the suppression of black rights, and Johnson's insistence that only the President could carry out Reconstruction increasingly caused Republican moderates to join with the Radicals against the President. The Republicans insisted, based on the Constitution's stipulations that Congress had the responsibility to guarantee "a republican form of government" and to admit new states to the Union, that the legislative branch, rather than the executive, should oversee Reconstruction. Johnson, however, attempted to block every move made by the Radicals. In February 1866, the Congress passed a law to enlarge the

Fortieth Congress.
Second Session.
In the House of Representatives, U.S.
March 2d 1868.

Articles

Exhibited by the House of Representatives of the United States, in the name of themselves and all the people of the United States, against Andrew Johnson, President of the United States, in maintenance and support of their impeachment against him for high crimes and misdemeanors in office.

Article 1.

That said Andrew Johnson President of the United States, on the twenty-first day of February, in the year of our Lord one thousand eight hundred and sixty-eight, at Washington, in the District of Columbia, unmindful of the high duties of his office, of his oath of office and of the requirement of the Constitution that he should take care that the laws be faithfully executed, did unlawfully, and in violation of the Constitution and laws of the United States, issue an order in writing for the removal of Edwin M. Stanton from the office of Secretary for the Department of War, said Edwin M. Stanton having been theretofore duly appointed and commissioned, by and with the advice and consent of the Senate of the United States, as such Secretary, and said Andrew Johnson, President of the United States, on the twelfth day of August, in the year of our Lord one thousand eight hundred and sixty-seven, and during the recess of said Senate, having suspended by his order Edwin M. Stanton from said office, and within twenty days after the first day of the next meeting of said Senate, that is to say, on the twelfth day of December in the year last afore-

The original articles of impeachment against President Andrew Johnson as sent by the House of Representatives to the Senate. (RG 46, National Archives) scope of the Freedmen's Bureau, which had been established to protect black rights in the South, and in April enacted a bill guaranteeing black civil rights. The President vetoed both laws, setting the stage for more dramatic conflicts to come.

In June, the Congress, after overriding Johnson's veto of the civil rights act, passed the 14th amendment to the Constitution against his opposition. The amendment, providing a federal guarantee of equal protection of the laws to all Americans, including the ex-slaves, now became a test of loyalty to the Union. Not surprisingly, all of the southern states reorganized by Johnson, except for Tennessee, rejected the amendment. This rejection, combined with deadly white riots against blacks in Memphis and New Orleans in May and July, convinced many northerners that Johnson's southern governments would not enforce civil rights. In addition, President Johnson's bitter and clumsy attacks against the Republicans in the fall congressional elections caused many voters to swing against the President. As a result, the number of Radical Republicans increased and the hand of Johnson's opponents was strengthened when Congress reconvened in December 1866.

Despite divisions between moderate and radical Republicans, they united in early 1867 against the Presidential program of Reconstruction. Congress, under a series of Reconstruction acts, the first of which was passed in March, abolished the state governments readmitted to the Union under Johnson and placed the South under military occupation. It also required the southern states, under the supervision of the U.S. Army, to hold elections in which blacks were allowed to vote while Confederate leaders were disenfranchised; the purpose of the elections was to choose representatives to state

The photograph shows the House of Representatives committee for the impeachment of Andrew Johnson. Left to right: Benjamin Butler (MA), James Wilson (IA), Thaddeus Stevens (PA), George Boutwell (MA), Thomas Williams (PA), John A. Logan (IL), and John A. Bingham (OH). (Mathew Brady, B-4371, National Archives)

conventions that would adopt new state constitutions and ratify the 14th amendment. Under this program, black political and civil rights became, for a brief period, the law of the land in the South.

President Johnson vehemently denounced Congressional Reconstruction as an unconstitutional interference in the affairs of what he considered to be sovereign states (as contrasted to the theory of some Radicals who considered the South a "conquered province" subject to federal reorganization). However, the strengthening of the Radical bloc in Congress now made it possible for the Republicans to pass their Reconstruction measures over his vetoes.

In response to Johnson's attempted obstruction of Congressional Reconstruction efforts, Congress passed in March 1867 the Tenure of Office Act, which required the President to gain the consent of the Senate in order to remove any officials he had previously appointed with the Senate's approval. It also passed the Army Appropriations Act, which required all military orders, even the President's, to go through General of the Army U.S. Grant. These measures, passed over Presidential vetoes and probably unconstitutional, successfully restricted the President's ability to interfere with Congressional Reconstruction.

At the same time, some Radicals, having decided to rid the government of a President they considered to be a traitor to the Union cause, began to press for Johnson's impeachment. The House set up a committee to investigate the President in early 1867, and by December the committee recommended impeachment. However, though the Republicans in Congress had united on the need for a new program of Reconstruction, not all agreed that Johnson's obstructionism merited impeachment. Radicals held that a broad construction of the "High Crimes and Misdemeanors" specification in the Constitution could include all misbehavior in office. This argument failed to convince the majority, who felt impeachment required a specific violation of federal or common law. The House rejected the committee's report by a vote of 100 to 57.

Only Johnson's removal of Radical Republican Edwin Stanton as Secretary of War, a clear violation of the Tenure of Office Act that Johnson instigated in order to test the law's constitutionality, finally convinced the House to vote for impeachment, 128 to 47, on February 24, 1868. On March 2 and 3 the House adopted 11 articles of impeachment against him. In these articles, the House charged that Johnson had deliberately violated the Tenure of Office Act and had attempted to subvert the Army Appropriation Act. In addition, the articles of impeachment charged the President with attempting to "bring into disgrace, ridicule, hatred, contempt, and reproach the Congress of the United States," specifying speeches he had made denouncing his congressional opponents during the election campaign of 1866.

The specific charges involved in the impeachment trial of Andrew Johnson seem trivial compared to the charges of subversion of civil and constitutional rights involved in the Watergate case more than 100 years later. Johnson's speeches constituted a political offense against the dominant party in Congress but bore no overtones of illegality, while the constitutionality and propriety of the Tenure of Office Act and the Army Appropriation Act remained highly doubtful. However, the real cause of the congressional collision with Johnson, as in the case of President Nixon, resulted not merely from the President's violation of a particular law but also from Congress' perception of a pattern of misuse of executive power by the President.

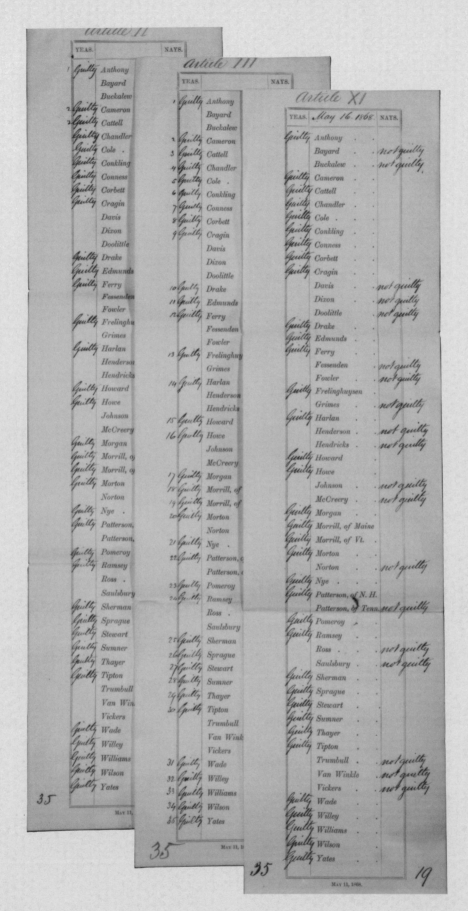

As shown on the three ballots used in the impeachment trial of President Andrew Johnson, March—May 1868, 35 senators voted for a "guilty" verdict and 19 voted "not guilty." Johnson was acquitted by one vote. (RG 46, National Archives)

The impeachment proceedings against President Johnson in the Senate, beginning on March 30 and lasting until May 16, established a number of important precedents. Among them, the Senate concluded that in its impeachment deliberations it would act similarly to a court of law, adhering to judicial standards of evidence and concentrating on specific Presidential violations of the law as grounds for conviction. The Senate agreed, for example, to have the Chief Justice of the Supreme Court settle all questions of law and evidence. This did not entirely change the political character of the proceedings, of course, for the decisions of the Chief Justice could still be overruled by a Senate vote, and Senators still had the power to vote for conviction regardless of the evidence. Nonetheless, Senate considerations during the trial focused on the legal technicalities of Johnson's alleged violation of the Tenure of Office Act and on the question of whether the act itself was constitutional, rather than on Johnson's opposition to Radical Reconstruction.

On May 16 the Senate began voting on article 11, which incorporated all of the charges against Johnson. It failed to convict. After an adjournment, the Senate voted on articles 2 and 3. In all three votes, 35 Senators voted "guilty" and 19 voted "not guilty." Lacking one vote of the two-thirds majority required to convict, the Senate adjourned the proceedings. Seven Republican Senators had voted repeatedly with the Democratic minority for acquittal, based on their belief in the unconstitutionality of the Tenure of Office Act as well as the fact that the law did not seem to apply to Cabinet officials or to the case of Secretary Stanton, appointed by Abraham Lincoln and therefore not subject to the act.

Though the Senate failed to convict and remove the President, supporters of impeachment had accomplished their main objective. Johnson had already lost his ability to control legislation in Congress; now he lost public credibility. Impeachment had succeeded for the moment in asserting legislative supremacy over an executive officer entirely out of sympathy with Congress. Finally, in the fall of 1868 the voters elected war hero U. S. Grant to the Presidency, placing in office a man unlikely to interfere with Congressional Reconstruction.

Based in part on the careful treatment accorded to the legal questions involved in Johnson's impeachment trial, during the Watergate hearings congressional investigators took special care to prove that the President had committed specific acts that violated his oath of office and therefore could be considered high crimes and misdemeanors. Due to the President's resignation, they never succeeded in bringing their evidence before the Senate. However, as in the case of the earlier proceedings against President Johnson, the initiation of impeachment proceedings against President Nixon provided an effective means for Congress to check what it considered to be illegal or unethical uses of power by the nation's highest official.

THE FACSIMILES

THE 11 ARTICLES OF IMPEACHMENT OF ANDREW JOHNSON PRINTED AS SENATE MISC. DOC. NO. 42. (Record Group 46, National Archives)

IN THE SENATE OF THE UNITED STATES.

ARTICLES OF IMPEACHMENT

EXHIBITED BY THE HOUSE OF REPRESENTATIVES AGAINST

ANDREW JOHNSON, PRESIDENT OF THE UNITED STATES.

MARCH 4, 1868.—Ordered to be printed.

FORTIETH CONGRESS, SECOND SESSION.

IN THE HOUSE OF REPRESENTATIVES UNITED STATES,
March 2, 1868

ARTICLES

Exhibited by the House of Representatives of the United States, in the name of themselves and all the people of the United States, against Andrew Johnson, President of the United States, in maintenance and support of their impeachment against him for high crimes and misdemeanors in office.

ARTICLE I.

That said Andrew Johnson, President of the United States, on the twenty-first day of February, in the year of our Lord one thousand eight hundred and sixty-eight, at Washington, in the District of Columbia, unmindful of the high duties of his office, of his oath of office, and of the requirement of the Constitution that he should take care that the laws be faithfully executed, did unlawfully, and in violation of the Constitution and laws of the United States, issue an order in writing for the removal of Edwin M. Stanton from the office of Secretary for the Department of War, said Edwin M. Stanton having been theretofore duly appointed and commissioned, by and with the advice and consent of the Senate of the United States, as such Secretary, and said Andrew Johnson, President of the United States, on the twelfth day of August, in the year of our Lord one thousand eight hundred and sixty-seven, and during the recess of said Senate, having suspended by his order Edwin M. Stanton from said office, and within twenty days after the first day of the next meeting of said Senate, that is to say, on the twelfth day of December in the year last aforesaid having reported to said Senate such suspension with the evidence and reasons for his action in the case and the name of the person designated to perform the duties of such office temporarily until the next meeting of the Senate, and said Senate thereafterwards on the thirteenth day of January, in the year of our Lord one thousand eight hundred and sixty-eight, having duly considered the evidence and reasons reported by said Andrew Johnson, for said suspension, and having refused to concur in said suspension, whereby and by force of the provisions of an act entitled "An act regulating the tenure of certain civil offices," passed

March second, eighteen hundred and sixty-seven, said Edwin M. Stanton did forthwith resume the functions of his office, whereof the said Andrew Johnson had then and there due notice, and said Edwin M. Stanton, by reason of the premises, on said twenty-first day of February, being lawfully entitled to hold said office of Secretary for the Department of War, which said order for the removal of said Edwin M. Stanton is in substance, as follows, that is to say:

EXECUTIVE MANSION,
Washington, D. C., February 21, 1868.

SIR: By virtue of the power and authority vested in me as President by the Constitution and laws of the United States you are hereby removed from office as Secretary for the Department of War, and your functions as such will terminate upon receipt of this communication.

You will transfer to Brevet Major General Lorenzo Thomas, Adjutant General of the army, who has this day been authorized and empowered to act as Secretary of War *ad interim,* all records, books, papers, and other public property now in your custody and charge.

Respectfully, yours,

ANDREW JOHNSON.

To the Hon. EDWIN M. STANTON, *Washington, D. C.*

Which order was unlawfully issued with intent then and there to violate the act entitled "An act regulating the tenure of certain civil offices," passed March second, eighteen hundred and sixty-seven, and with the further intent, contrary to the provisions of said act, in violation thereof, and contrary to the provisions of the Constitution of the United States, and without the advice and consent of the Senate of the United States, the said Senate then and there being in session, to remove said Edwin M. Stanton from the office of Secretary for the Department of War, the said Edwin M. Stanton, being then and there Secretary for the Department of War, and being then and there in the due and lawful execution and discharge of the duties of said office, whereby said Andrew Johnson, President of the United States, did then and there commit, and was guilty of a high misdemeanor in office.

ARTICLE II.

That on said twenty-first day of February, in the year of our Lord one thousand eight hundred and sixty-eight, at Washington, in the District of Columbia, said Andrew Johnson, President of the United States, unmindful of the high duties of his office, of his oath of office, and in violation of the Constitution of the United States, and contrary to the provisions of an act entitled "An act regulating the tenure of certain civil offices," passed March second, eighteen hundred and sixty-seven, without the advice and consent of the Senate of the United States, said Senate then and there being in session, and without authority of law, did, with intent to violate the Constitution of the United States, and the act aforesaid, issue and deliver to one Lorenzo Thomas a letter of authority in substance as follows, that is to say:

EXECUTIVE MANSION,
Washington, D. C., February 21, 1868.

SIR: The Hon. Edwin M. Stanton having been this day removed from office as Secretary for the Department of War, you are hereby authorized and empowered to act as Secretary of War *ad interim,* and will immediately enter upon the discharge of the duties pertaining to that office.

Mr. Stanton has been instructed to transfer to you all the records, books, papers, and other public property now in his custody and charge.

Respectfully, yours,

ANDREW JOHNSON.

To Brevet Major General LORENZO THOMAS,
Adjutant General U. S. Army, Washington, D. C.

Then and there being no vacancy in said office of Secretary for the Department of War, whereby said Andrew Johnson, President of the United States, did then and there commit, and was guilty of a high misdemeanor in office.

ARTICLE III.

That said Andrew Johnson, President of the United States, on the twenty-first day of February, in the year of our Lord one thousand eight hundred and sixty-eight, at Washington, in the District of Columbia, did commit and was guilty of a high misdemeanor in office in this, that, without authority of law, while the Senate of the United States was then and there in session, he did appoint one Lorenzo Thomas to be Secretary for the Department of War *ad interim*, without the advice and consent of the Senate, and with intent to violate the Constitution of the United States, no vacancy having happened in said office of Secretary for the Department of War during the recess of the Senate, and no vacancy existing in said office at the time, and which said appointment, so made by said Andrew Johnson, of said Lorenzo Thomas, is in substance as follows, that is to say:

EXECUTIVE MANSION,
Washington, D. C., February 21, 1868.

SIR: The Hon. Edwin M. Stanton having been this day removed from office as Secretary for the Department of War, you are hereby authorized and empowered to act as Secretary of War *ad interim*, and will immediately enter upon the discharge of the duties pertaining to that office.

Mr. Stanton has been instructed to transfer to you all the records, books, papers, and other public property now in his custody and charge.

Respectfully yours,

ANDREW JOHNSON.

To Brevet Major General LORENZO THOMAS,
Adjutant General U. S. Army, Washington, D. C.

ARTICLE IV.

That said Andrew Johnson, President of the United States, unmindful of the high duties of his office and of his oath of office, in violation of the Constitution and laws of the United States, on the twenty-first day of February, in the year of our Lord one thousand eight hundred and sixty-eight, at Washington, in the District of Columbia, did unlawfully conspire with one Lorenzo Thomas, and with other persons to the House of Representatives unknown, with intent, by intimidation and threats, unlawfully to hinder and prevent Edwin M. Stanton, then and there the Secretary for the Department of War, duly appointed under the laws of the United States, from holding said office of Secretary for the Department of War, contrary to and in violation of the Constitution of the United States, and of the provisions of an act entitled "An act to define and punish certain conspiracies," approved July thirty-first, eighteen hundred and sixty-one, whereby said Andrew Johnson, President of the United States, did then and there commit and was guilty of a high crime in office.

ARTICLE V.

That said Andrew Johnson, President of the United States, unmindful of the high duties of his office and of his oath of office, on the twenty-first day of February, in the year of our Lord one thousand eight hundred and sixty-eight, and on divers other days and times in said year, before the second day of March, in the year of our Lord one thousand eight hundred and sixty-eight, at Washington, in the District of Columbia, did unlawfully conspire with one Lorenzo Thomas, and with other persons to the House of Representatives unknown, to prevent and hinder the execution of an act entitled "An act regulating the tenure of certain civil offices," passed March second, eighteen hundred and sixty-seven, and in pursuance of said conspiracy, did unlawfully attempt to prevent Edwin M. Stanton, then and there being Secretary for the Department of War, duly appointed and commissioned under the laws of the United States, from holding said office, whereby the said Andrew Johnson, President of the United States, did then and there commit and was guilty of a high misdemeanor in office.

ARTICLE VI.

That said Andrew Johnson, President of the United States, unmindful of the high duties of his office and of his oath of office, on the twenty-first day of February, in the year of our Lord one thousand eight hundred and sixty-eight, at Washington, in the District of Columbia, did unlawfully conspire with one Lorenzo Thomas, by force to seize, take, and possess the property of the United States in the Department of War, and then and there in the custody and charge of Edwin M. Stanton, Secretary for said Department, contrary to the provisions of an act entitled "An act to define and punish certain conspiracies," approved July thirty-one, eighteen hundred and sixty-one, and with intent to violate and disregard an act entitled "An act regulating the tenure of certain civil offices," passed March second, eighteen hundred and sixty-seven, whereby said Andrew Johnson, President of the United States, did then and there commit a high crime in office.

ARTICLE VII.

That said Andrew Johnson, President of the United States, unmindful of the high duties of his office and of his oath of office, on the twenty-first day of February, in the year of our Lord one thousand eight hundred and sixty-eight, at Washington, in the District of Columbia, did unlawfully conspire with one Lorenzo Thomas with intent unlawfully to seize, take, and possess the property of the United States in the Department of War, in the custody and charge of Edwin M. Stanton, Secretary for said Department, with intent to violate and disregard the act entitled "An act regulating the tenure of certain civil offices," passed March second, eighteen hundred and sixty-seven, whereby said Andrew Johnson, President of the United States, did then and there commit a high misdemeanor in office.

ARTICLE VIII.

That said Andrew Johnson, President of the United States, unmindful of the high duties of his office, and of his oath of office, with intent unlawfully to control the disbursements of the moneys appropriated for the military service and for the Department of War, on the twenty-first day of February, in the year of our Lord one thousand eight hundred and sixty-eight, at Washington, in the District of Columbia, did unlawfully and contrary to the provisions of an act entitled "An act regulating the tenure of certain civil offices," passed March second, eighteen hundred and sixty-seven, and in violation of the Constitution of the United States, and without the advice and consent of the Senate of the United States, and while the Senate was then and there in session, there being no vacancy in the office of Secretary for the Department of War, and with intent to violate and disregard the act aforesaid, then and there issue and deliver to one Lorenzo Thomas a letter of authority in writing, in substance as follows, that is to say:

EXECUTIVE MANSION,
Washington, D. C., February 21, 1868.

SIR: The Hon. Edwin M. Stanton having been this day removed from office as Secretary for the Department of War, you are hereby authorized and empowered to act as Secretary of War *ad interim*, and will immediately enter upon the discharge of the duties pertaining to that office.

Mr. Stanton has been instructed to transfer to you all the records, books, papers, and other public property now in his custody and charge.

Respectfully yours,

ANDREW JOHNSON

To Brevet Major General LORENZO THOMAS,
Adjutant General U. S. Army, Washington, D. C.

Whereby said Andrew Johnson, President of the United States, did then and there commit and was guilty of a high misdemeanor in office.

ARTICLE IX.

That said Andrew Johnson, President of the United States, on the twenty-second day of February, in the year of our Lord one thousand eight hundred and sixty-eight, at Washington, in the District of Columbia, in disregard of the Constitution and the laws of the United States duly enacted, as commander-in-chief of the army of the United States, did bring before himself then and there William H. Emory, a major general by brevet in the army of the United States, actually in command of the Department of Washington and the military forces thereof, and did then and there, as such commander-in-chief, declare to and instruct said Emory that part of a law of the United States, passed March second, eighteen hundred and sixty-seven, entitled " An act making appropriations for the support of the army for the year ending June thirtieth, eighteen hundred and sixty-eight, and for other purposes," especially the second section thereof, which provides, among other things, that " all orders and instructions relating to military operations issued by the President or Secretary of War shall be issued through the General of the army, and, in case of his inability through the next in rank " was unconstitutional, and in contravention of the commission of said Emory, and which said provision of law had been theretofore duly and legally promulgated by General Order for the government and direction of the army of the United States, as the said Andrew Johnson then and there well knew, with intent thereby to induce said Emory in his official capacity as commander of the Department of Washington, to violate the provisions of said act, and to take and receive, act upon, and obey such orders as he, the said Andrew Johnson, might make and give, and which should not be issued through the General of the Army of the United States, according to the provisions of said act, and with the further intent thereby to enable him, the said Andrew Johnson, to prevent the execution of the act entiled " An act regulating the tenure of certain civil offices," passed March second, eighteen hundred and sixty-seven, and to unlawfully prevent Edwin M. Stanton, then being Secretary for the Department of War, from holding said office and discharging the duties thereof, whereby said Andrew Johnson, President of the United States, did then and there commit and was guilty of a high misdemeanor in office.

And the House of Representatives, by protestation, saving to themselves the liberty of exhibiting at any time hereafter any further articles or other accusation, or impeachment against the said Andrew Johnson, President of the United States, and also of replying to his answers which he shall make unto the articles herein preferred against him, and of offering proof to the same, and every part thereof, and to all and every other article, accusation, or impeachment which shall be exhibited by them, as the case shall require, DO DEMAND that the said Andrew Johnson may be put to answer the high crimes and misdemeanors in office herein charged against him, and that such proceedings, examinations, trials, and judgments may be thereupon had and given as may be agreeable to law and justice.

SCHUYLER COLFAX,
Speaker of the House of Representatives.

Attest:
EDWARD McPHERSON,
Clerk of the House of Representatives.

IN THE HOUSE OF REPRESENTATIVES UNITED STATES,
March 3, 1868.

The following additional articles of impeachment were agreed to, viz :

ARTICLE X.

That said Andrew Johnson, President of the United States, unmindful of the high duties of his office and the dignity and proprieties thereof, and of the harmony and courtesies which ought to exist and be maintained between the executive and legislative branches of the government of the United States, designing and intending to set aside the rightful authority and powers of Congress, did attempt to bring into disgrace, ridicule, hatred, contempt and reproach the Congress of the United States, and the several branches thereof, to impair and destroy the regard and respect of all the good people of the United States for the Congress and legislative power thereof, (which all officers of the government ought inviolably to preserve and maintain,) and to excite the odium and resentment of all the good people of the United States against Congress and the laws by it duly and constitutionally enacted ; and in pursuance of his said design and intent, openly and publicly, and before divers assemblages of the citizens of the United States convened in divers parts thereof to meet and receive said Andrew Johnson as the Chief Magistrate of the United States, did, on the eighteenth day of August, in the year of our Lord one thousand eight hundred and sixty-six, and on divers other days and times, as well before as afterward, make and deliver with a loud voice certain intemperate, inflammatory and scandalous harangues, and did therein utter loud threats and bitter menaces as well against Congress as the laws of the United States duly enacted thereby, amid the cries, jeers and laughter of the multitudes then assembled and in hearing, which are set forth in the several specifications hereinafter written, in substance and effect, that is to say :

SPECIFICATION FIRST.—In this, that at Washington, in the District of Columbia, in the Executive Mansion, to a committee of citizens who called upon the President of the United States, speaking of and concerning the Congress of the United States, said Andrew Johnson, President of the United States, heretofore, to wit, on the eighteenth day of August, in the year of our Lord one thousand eight hundred and sixty-six, did, in a loud voice, declare in substance and effect, among other things, that is to say :

"So far as the Executive Department of the government is concerned, the effort has been made to restore the Union, to heal the breach, to pour oil into the wounds which were consequent upon the struggle, and (to speak in common phrase) to prepare as the learned and wise physician would, a plaster healing in character and coextensive with the wound. We thought, and we think, that we had partially succeeded ; but as the work progresses, as reconstruction seemed to be taking place, and the country was becoming reunited, we found a disturbing and marring element opposing us. In alluding to that element, I shall go no further than your convention and the distinguished gentleman who has delivered to me the report of its proceedings. I shall make no reference to it that I do not believe the time and the occasion justify.

"We have witnessed in one department of the government every endeavor to prevent the restoration of peace, harmony, and Union. We have seen hanging upon the verge of the government, as it were, a body called, or which assumes to be, the Congress of the United States, while in fact it is a Congress of only a part of the States. We have seen this Congress pretend to be for the Union, when its every step and act tended to perpetuate disunion and make a disruption of the States inevitable.   *   *   *   We have seen Congress gradually encroach step by step upon constitutional rights, and violate, day after day and month after month, fundamental principles of the government. We have seen a Congress that seemed to forget that there was a limit to the sphere and scope of legislation. We have seen a Congress in a minority assume to exercise power which, allowed to be consummated, would result in despotism or monarchy itself."

SPECIFICATION SECOND. In this, that at Cleveland, in the State of Ohio, heretofore, to wit, on the third day of September, in the year of our Lord one thousand eight hundred and sixty-six, before a public assemblage of citizens and others, said Andrew Johnson, President of the United States, speaking of and concerning the Congress of the United States did, in a loud voice, declare in substance and effect among other things, that is to say:

"I will tell you what I did do. I called upon your Congress that is trying to break up the government."

* * * * * * * * *

"In conclusion, beside that, Congress had taken much pains to poison their constituents against him. But what had Congress done? Have they done anything to restore the union of these States? No: on the contrary, they had done everything to prevent it; and because he stood now where he did when the rebellion commenced, he had been denounced as a traitor. Who had run greater risks or made greater sacrifices than himself? But Congress, factious and domineering, had undertaken to poison the minds of the American people."

SPECIFICATION THIRD.—In this, that at St. Louis, in the State of Missouri, heretofore, to wit, on the eighth day of September, in the year of our Lord one thousand eight hundred and sixty-six, before a public assemblage of citizens and others, said Andrew Johnson, President of the United States, speaking of and concerning the Congress of the United States, did, in a loud voice, declare, in substance and effect, among other things, that is to say:

"Go on. Perhaps if you had a word or two on the subject of New Orleans you might understand more about it than you do. And if you will go back—if you will go back and ascertain the cause of the riot at New Orleans perhaps you will not be so prompt in calling out 'New Orleans.' If you will take up the riot at New Orleans, and trace it back to its source or its immediate cause, you will find out who was responsible for the blood that was shed there. If you will take up the riot at New Orleans and trace it back to the radical Congress, you will find that the riot at New Orleans was substantially planned. If you will take up the proceedings in their caucuses you will understand that they there knew that a convention was to be called which was extinct by its power having expired; that it was said that the intention was that a new government was to be organized, and on the organization of that government the intention was to enfranchise one portion of the population, called the colored population, who had just been emancipated, and at the same time disfranchise white men. When you design to talk about New Orleans you ought to understand what you are talking about. When you read the speeches that were made, and take up the facts on the Friday and Saturday before that convention sat, you will there find that speeches were made incendiary in their character, exciting that portion of the population, the black population, to arm themselves and prepare for the shedding of blood. You will also find that that convention did assemble in violation of law, and the intention of that convention was to supersede the reorganized authorities in the State government of Louisiana, which had been recognized by the government of the United States; and every man engaged in that rebellion in that convention, with the intention of superseding and upturning the civil government which had been recognized by the government of the United States, I say that he was a traitor to the Constitution of the United States, and hence you find that another rebellion was commenced, *having its origin in the radical Congress.*"

* * * * * * * * *

"So much for the New Orleans riot. And there was the cause and the origin of the blood that was shed; and every drop of blood that was shed is upon their skirts, and they are responsible for it. I could test this thing a little closer, but will not do it here to-night. But when you talk about the causes and consequences that resulted from proceedings of that kind, perhaps, as I have been introduced here, and you have provoked questions of this kind, though it does not provoke me, I will tell you a few wholesome things that have been done by this radical Congress in connection with New Orleans and the extension of the elective franchise.

"I know that I have been traduced and abused. I know it has come in advance of me here as elsewhere—that I have attempted to exercise an arbitrary power in resisting laws that were intended to be forced upon the government; that I had exercised that power; that I had abandoned the party that elected me, and that I was a traitor, because I exercised the veto power in attempting, and did arrest for a time, a bill that was called a "Freedman's Bureau" bill; yes, that I was a traitor. And I have been traduced, I have been slandered, I have been maligned, I have been called Judas Iscariot and all that. Now, my countrymen, here to-night, it is very easy to indulge in epithets; it is easy to call a man Judas and cry out traitor, but when he is called upon to give arguments and facts he is very often found wanting. Judas Iscariot—Judas. There was a Judas, and he was one of the twelve apostles. Oh! yes, the twelve apostles had a Christ. The twelve apostles had a Christ, and he never could have had a Judas unless he had had twelve apostles. If I have played the Judas, who has been my Christ that I have played the Judas with? Was it Thad. Stevens? Was it Wendell Phillips? Was it Charles Sumner? These are the men that stop and compare themselves with the Saviour; and everybody that differs with them in opinion, and to try to stay and arrest their diabolical and nefarious policy, is to be denounced as a Judas."

* * * * * * * * *

"Well, let me say to you, if you will stand by me in this action, if you will stand by me in trying to give the people a fair chance—soldiers and citizens—to participate in these offices, God being willing, I will kick them out. I will kick them out just as fast as I can.

"Let me say to you, in concluding, that what I have said I intended to say. I was not provoked into this, and I care not for their menaces, the taunts, and the jeers. I care not for threats. I do not intend to be bullied by my enemies nor overawed by my friends. But, God willing, with your help, I will veto their measures whenever any of them come to me.' '

Which said utterances, declarations, threats, and harangues, highly censurable in any, are peculiarly indecent and unbecoming in the Chief Magistrate of the United States, by means whereof said Andrew Johnson has brought the high office of the President of the United States into contempt, ridicule, and disgrace, to the great scandal of all good citizens, whereby said Andrew Johnson, President of the United States, did commit, and was then and there guilty of a high misdemeanor in office.

ARTICLE XI.

That said Andrew Johnson, President of the United States, unmindful of the high duties of his office, and of his oath of office, and in disregard of the Constitution and laws of the United States, did, heretofore, to wit, on the eighteenth day of August, A. D. eighteen hundred and sixty-six, at the city of Washington, and the District of Columbia, by public speech, declare and affirm, in substance, that the thirty-ninth Congress of the United States was not a Congress of the United States authorized by the Constitution to exercise legislative power under the same, but, on the contrary, was a Congress of only part of the States, thereby denying, and intending to deny, that the legislation of said Congress was valid or obligatory upon him, the said Andrew Johnson, except in so far as he saw fit to approve the same, and also thereby denying, and intending to deny, he power of the said thirty-ninth Congress to propose amendments to the Constitution of the United States; and, in pursuance of said declaration, the said Andrew Johnson, President of the United States, afterwards, to wit, on the twenty-first day of February, A. D. eighteen hundred and sixty-eight, at the city of Washington, in the District of Columbia, did, unlawfully, and in disregard of the requirement of the Constitution, that he should take care that the laws be faithfully executed, attempt to prevent the execution of an act entitled "An act regulating the tenure of certain civil offices," passed March second, eighteen hundred and sixty-seven, by unlawfully devising and contriving, and attempting to devise and contrive means by which he should prevent Edwin M. Stanton from forthwith resuming the functions of the office of Secretary for the Department of War, notwithstanding the refusal of the Senate to concur in the suspension theretofore made by said Andrew Johnson of said Edwin M. Stanton from said office of Secretary for the Department of War; and, also, by further unlawfully devising and contriving, and attempting to devise and contrive means, then and there, to prevent the execution of an act entitled "An act making appropriations for the support of the army for the fiscal year ending June thirtieth, eighteen hundred and sixty-eight, and for other purposes," approved March second, eighteen hundred and sixty-seven; and, also, to prevent the execution of an act entitled "An act to provide for the more efficient government of the rebel States," passed March second, eighteen hundred and sixty seven, whereby the said Andrew Johnson, President of the United States, did, then, to wit, on the twenty-first day of February, A. D. eighteen hundred and sixty-eight, at the city of Washington, commit, and was guilty of, a high misdemeanor in office.

SCHUYLER COLFAX,
Speaker of the House of Representatives.

Attest:
EDWARD MCPHERSON,
Clerk of the House of Representatives.